Hinds' Feet on High Places

(Children's Version)

Family Activity Guide

by

Sandra Held

This book is dedicated to my precious children!

Darcy

Todd

Tim

Tory

Nicole

&

Hailee

About the Author

I am a rural Nebraska wife of a carpenter, home school mother of 6 children. I have 2 married children and 2 grandchildren so far. I love outdoor activities including gardening, camping, turkey hunting, canoeing, and dutch oven cooking.

Besides penning this book, I have designed a "Key to My Heart" purity ring for girls, and a "God's Timing" watch for boys. With several other projects in the making, I have incorporated them into a business called A.I.M. Enterprises. A.I.M. stands for Articles Inspiring Maturity. My website can be found at www.aim4theheart.com.

A special thank you to those who inspired and
encouraged me to write this book!
Shelley, Trace, and Carol for prodding me to do this.
Janice and Kevin for proof-reading.
Melinda for her beautiful artwork on the cover
and throughout the book.
My husband, Dean, for encouraging me to write
and giving me his blessing to do this.
And my family for being patient and very helpful
through this process.
Many dear friends who pray for and love me.
And to my Awesome God who has taken me tot he
Heights as well!

~ I love you all ~

Table of Contents

Introduction

This book was written to enhance the lessons in <u>Hind's Feet on High Places</u> (Illustrated) with the intent of taking your children to the high places with the main character, Much-Afraid. You and your children will be actively participating with her on this journey. Keep this thought in mind as you go through this book and continually remind your children that God is doing a mighty work in their hearts as you proceed. Keep in constant prayer for them and even journal your own thoughts in your secret place. God has a very special task for you at the end of this journey! As you pray for each child, consider their personalities and the character God is developing in their precious lives.

To make this devotional special and meaningful please make sure you are well prepared ahead of time, having gathered and assembled all your supplies. Receiving tokens along the way and putting things into practice are what makes this journey so special for each child. They feel like they are actually participating with Much-Afraid on her journey.

May God richly bless you as you lead your children on their own spiritual journeys to the High Places!

Sandra Held

Supplies needed to complete the activities:

A copy of Hinds Feet on High Places (Illustrated) by Dian Layton
journals (for the older ones)
(or create your own using pages in Part Two of this book as
examples)
colored highlight markers
a Bible per child
a small pouch per child (see page 47)
6 (walnut to golf-ball sized) stones per child
stone cards copied on cardstock from page 89 (1 page per child)
small jar of sand per child (about the size of a baby food jar)
small jar per child of ½ whole wheat flour and ½ wheat kernels
candles and tea lights
a small piece of pottery or clay for each child to fashion into a dish
jar of anointing oil   (olive oil or Vitamin E oil works fine)
1 bag of large marshmallows
colored poster board (gold is ideal but not necessary)

This book will take you through Hinds' Feet on High Places
(Illustrated) in 28 days with lots of fun-filled activities to deepen the
spiritual lessons found therein. There is a list of needed supplies at the
beginning of each chapter so that you can be well prepared for fun and
great spiritual intimacy with your family. Children from preschool
through junior high will enjoy this story. There are activities for all in
varying degrees of participation.

Pre-assembled kits
available at
www.aim4theheart.com

Part One

Daily

Devotions

<u>**Supplies needed for Chapter 1**</u>
Per child:
     Bible
     Journal
     (Or create your own using example journal pages in Part Two of this book)
     Supplies for secret places. (See Day 4 for details)

<u>*Day 1*</u>

Chapter 1
"In the Village of Much-Trembling"

Read page 1-11.

Start off by looking at the picture of the Village of Humiliation. Have children describe what they think it must be like to live there. Poor, noisy, unruly children, hard work, etc. Explain what humiliation means. Ask older ones to look it up in the dictionary. Make sure they understand the difference between humiliation and humbleness.

After reading the story discuss the "Think About It" section on Page 11.

Day 2

Putting it into Practice

Give each child a small journal and a highlighter or make a journal for each child, using the pages in the back of this book as examples and adding to it as you progress. A small 3-ring binder or a 3-prong pocket folder works well for this. Have them look up the verses in their Bibles, highlight them and copy them into their journals.

1 Samuel 16:7
Psalm 18:33
Habakkuk 3:19
Psalm 18:3

This is a great way to get them familiar with their Bibles. Highlighting gives them ease in finding verses they know they have studied before and helps personalize their Bibles. Writing them out helps plant the seeds of God's Word a little deeper in their hearts.
Pray the prayer together on Page 12. This is also written on the corresponding journal page.

All prayers in the devotional book are also included in the journal pages at the back of this book. Older children can write their own prayers similar to the ones in the corresponding book.

Day 3

Read aloud page 13-20.
Discuss the "Think about it" section.

Memorize **Matthew 6:6** and record in your journals. Keep it simple for the little ones. Have children learn it in the version of your choice. Make place mats for the table with the verse on it and say it as a family before each meal. Be creative! You could use construction paper, paint, markers, stickers, paper doilies, or old greeting cards. Then cover with clear contact paper.

The prayer is on Day 3 Journal page also.

Matthew 6:6
But when you pray, go into your room, close the door and pray to your Father, who is unseen. Then your Father, who sees what is done in secret, will reward you!

Day 4

Putting it into Practice

Create your own secret place.

Have fun with this!

Have each child pick out a special place in the house where they can create their own secret place to meet with the Lord each day!

My 9-year-old daughter set up a little area behind the couch which set at an angle in our living room. She put a little stand back there with a lamp on it, a cross, her Bible, journal, pen and highlighter. She also had throw pillows, a blanket and a stuffed sheep in her secret place to make it comfortable and cozy. My son, age 11, just used a nook in his room with a bean bag chair and a lamp on a small stand which he had built, keeping his supplies on shelves underneath the lamp.

The purpose of the secret place is to encourage our children to spend quiet time with the Lord by themselves each day! We used this special place to work on our journals and to pray. Also, it is a great place to keep the mementos they will receive along the way.

Supplies needed for Chapter 2

cards to send to those in need of encouragement
a meal or snack for someone in need of encouragement
paper to make posters for secret places

Day 5

Chapter 2
"Beginning the Journey"

Read page 23-32 and do the "Think About It" section.

Have you ever thought about the possibility of God using Sorrow and Suffering in your life as companions to bring you closer to Him? If you think about it, that is exactly what He does. We never need the Lord as much as we do when we endure sorrow and suffering. That is when our hearts are the most tender toward Him, and when He can accomplish much healing and grant strength and wisdom to us. Hopefully we will view sorrow and suffering this way from now on and draw ever closer to our Lord rather than push Him away when we need Him most.

Assign journal work in their secret places using the verses on Page 32. Look up the verses in their Bibles, highlight them and write them in their journals. You may have older ones write comments on what each verse means to them if you want to incorporate some creative or persuasive writing skills into this project.

Pray the prayer for this day as you spend time in your "secret place."

Day 6

Putting it into practice

Pray for those you know who are suffering and going through a time of trouble. Send a card, or make a meal or snack to cheer up someone in your neighborhood, church family or local nursing home.

Discuss again what you learned from yesterday's reading. Review helps them remember and apply it better. Discuss the importance of putting their faith to action, thus the reason for ministering to someone in need of cheering up! Start a prayer list in their journals.

Day 7

Read aloud page 33-38 and do the "Think About It" section.

Recall the stories and discuss how pride was demonstrated in the following Bible characters:

Adam and Eve - Genesis 2:4-3:24

Samson - Judges 13-16

Saul - 1 Samuel 9 -19

Solomon - 1 Kings 2- 11

Encourage conversation, not just passive listening to what you have to say. Learn to bring out the deep thoughts in your children and teach them to express their hearts.

Day 8

Putting it into Practice

Work on the memory verse, **Proverbs 16:18** in the version of your choice. Make it into a small poster to hang in their secret place, and there have them pray the prayer in their journal for this day. Encourage older ones to journal their thoughts about Much-Afraid's journey.

Supplies needed for Chapter 3

 one small cloth pouch per child (see instructions on page 47)
 a copy of page 89 on cardstock, one page per child
 3 walnut-sized stones per child
 stones and tea light for a mini altar centerpiece
 (instructions on page 48)
 one small jar of sand per child labeled
 "God will provide even in the desert"
 a little cross to go inside the jar of sand
 a small artificial sunflower per child (optional)
 one small jar ½ full of whole wheat flour and ½ full of wheat kernels
 You will be making a loaf of bread from scratch so find your favorite recipe and have the ingredients ready.
 a small pottery vase or clay for each child to make a finger- ring dish or small vase

Day 9

Chapter 3
"Through the Desert and Loneliness"

Read page 41 thru very top of page 44.
You will give each child a pouch at this time.
(Directions on page 47)

Have them find a small stone outside or collect some ahead of time. Make sure the stones are big enough to write the word **"trust"** with a permanent marker on them. Then give card # 1 along with it to keep in the outside pocket of their pouch. Have each child keep his pouch in his secret place.

As a family, build a mini altar with stones and a candle in the middle. (A suggestion for one is found on page 48.) Discuss trusting God in all things. Share a time when you had to trust God in an uncertain circumstance or incorporate the trust thought into something going on in someone's life near to them. Use people and circumstances around you to illustrate lessons along the way. As a family, choose to lay down your desires and accept God's total leading in all areas of your life. Light the candle and gather around the altar, committing this decision to prayer. It will be very meaningful for all of you. Make the altar the centerpiece of your dining room table and light it during meals. It will be a constant reminder of the commitment you made and will make a wonderful conversation piece for company, giving you a chance to share what God is doing in your family through this study and His Word.

Days 10 and 11

Read from the top of page 44 thru the first four paragraphs. **".....after this, the Shepherd took her back to the huts to rest for the night."** End there for today.

Briefly read and review the following "desert" Bible stories. Take more than one day to dig deeper if you wish to.

Abraham and Sarah

Genesis17:15-16: 21:1-7 God kept His promise to Abraham and gave him a son, even though Sarah was way too old to have a baby. He wants us to trust Him with the things that look impossible to us. Jesus said, "Nothing shall be impossible for you." That shows us that situations may come that will appear impossible to us. They are opportunities to trust God.

Joseph

Genesis 37 Joseph was sold as a slave by his own brothers.
Genesis 39 Joseph was unjustly thrown into prison by a woman's lies. But God was with him and gave him success in whatever he did.
Genesis 41:41-56 Pharaoh put Joseph in charge of all of Egypt. He became a powerful and wise leader. In **Genesis 45** Joseph is restored to his family and his father is overjoyed! This is a wonderful story of how much God cares for us, protects us and uses us in very difficult circumstances. He will always use the circumstances in our lives for our good and for His glory!

Moses and the Children of Israel

Exodus 16 & 17 The children of Israel learned to trust God to supply their food and water while in the desert after brought them out of Egypt. What food did He supply for them?

Jesus

Luke 4:1-13 Several times in the desert, the devil did his best to tempt Jesus, but God strengthened Him, not with food and water but with the Holy Spirit and He prevailed. He strengthens us with the same Holy Spirit to stand against the devil and to do what pleases our Heavenly Father. We need to constantly recognize and utilize that strength that can only come from the Holy Spirit.

Give to each child a small jar of sand labeled:

"God will Provide even in the Desert"

as a reminder for his or her secret place. Have each child put the little cross in his jar of sand and shake it up. This symbolizes that, though we may not always see Him, Jesus is with us continually, even in the desert times.

Pray with them about the dry times in their lives when they will have to trust God in some hard circumstances.

Spend time in your secret place asking God to fill you with His Holy Spirit and to strengthen you with His power so you can stand firm against the temptations of the devil and do what pleases God!

Day 12

Begin reading the 5th paragraph on page 44 starting where you left off last time. "In the morning . . ." thru page 45, the first paragraph.

Putting it into practice

This is a story of the process of making grain into flour and then into bread. Give jars of flour and grain to remind children to allow God to use them to feed others. Label them **"Feed Others With Kindness"**. Our kind deeds and words "feed" a person encouragement who is in need of it. Pray that they would find great delight in being used of Him and be willing for him to fashion them into whoever He wants them to be. In their secret places have them ask the Lord who He wants them to bless and encourage. Who needs to be fed a kind word and how can He use them to do it?

Highlight and write in journals the following verses

Isaiah 28:28a
Luke 22:31-32

Make homemade bread and share it with someone. Include a blessing card with it! Feed them kindness with your gift of bread and words!

Day 13

Read aloud page 45, second paragraph thru page 46, second paragraph.

Putting it into Practice

Give to each child a small pottery vase or a piece of clay they can fashion into a ring dish to hold their "gold." As they mold and shape it into what they want it to become, have them consider that God is doing the same thing in their lives. After they bake it (fire it) in the oven and decorate it as they see fit, remind them that God must put us in the oven of fiery trials to seal us the way he has designed us. The decorating we have in our lives is the good things we do as a result of loving and serving our Lord.

Show your wedding ring and if you have access to some unrefined gold, observe the changes in the gold from its natural state to the ring as a result of the refining process. What a great visual of the process in us as God refines our character!

A trip to a pottery shop would be great too!

Do whatever you can to deepen this lesson for them!

Suggested songs to sing:

"Change my Heart, Oh God"
"The Potter's Hand" by Darlene Zschech

Day 14

Putting it into Practice

Highlight and copy the following verses in your journals as you spend time in your secret place.

Gold   Malachi 3:3
**   Job 23:10**

Clay   Isaiah 64:8
**   Jeremiah 18:3-6**
**   1 Peter 4:12-13**
**   James 1:2**

The trials we go through in life are like the fiery furnace that purifies and strengthens our faith through testing. We will be overjoyed when God's glory is revealed! Be sure to reward their hard work tomorrow and review the verses, helping them to see God's wisdom pouring through them into their hearts.

This is a lot of journal work for the older ones, but so important. Help them find delight in being in God's Word. They could listen to a praise tape while doing their secret place work if possible. Younger ones would at least be able to look up and highlight the verses in their Bibles. Pray for a love of God's Word!

Day 15

Finish reading the rest of this chapter. Pages 46-47.

Do the "Think About It" section on page 48.
(They have already put these verses in their journals.)

Putting it into Practice

An artificial sunflower to put in the top of their jar of sand or in their pottery dish would be a nice finishing touch to this lesson, pointing out that we can bloom and be beautiful for Jesus wherever He places us! Even in the dry places!

Also gather the second stone and write **"Acceptance with Joy"** on it. Give the labeled stone and second card to each child..

They made it through the fiery trial of **"Much Writing"** and hopefully they did it as **Acceptance-With-Joy!**

Discuss the tokens given so far and what they mean to them.

Encourage them to spend time in your secret places and pray the prayer in their journals from page 49 in the book.

Day 16

Read aloud page 50 - 55.

Putting it into Practice

Present stone #3 **"Wait Patiently"** and the 3rd card saying, **"I will wait patiently until the Lord does what He said He will do"**

Discuss waiting patiently. Have children describe what it is like to wait patiently. Do they listen to Resentment, Bitterness, and Self-Pity? Talk about what these mean. How do they hinder us from waiting patiently?

Share your own experiences when you have struggled with these things too! God gave us emotions, but not to lead and guide us. We can't help what emotions we feel, but we don't let them control us. We control our response to our feelings. We can choose to wait patiently no matter how impatient we feel.

Day 17

Read aloud page 56-58
Discuss the "Think About It" section.

Putting it into Practice

Highlight the memory verse in Bibles and record it in journals.
Make a bookmark with **Proverbs 3:5** on it and decorate to your own
taste! Use this as a reminder to memorize this verse.
Say the prayer together or individually in their secret places.

Supplies needed for Chapter 4

> **3 stones per child**
> **cards numbered: 4, 5, and 6 (1 of each per child)**
> **decorative jar of anointing oil (olive or Vitamin E oil)**
> **Label it "Spirit of Grace and Comfort"**
> **1 red flower per child**

Day 18

Chapter 4
"Up the Mountain of Injury"

Read Aloud pages 61-67
Discuss the "Think About It" section.

Putting it into Practice

Present the 4th stone with the words **"Your Will, Lord"**
written on it and the 4th card to each child.
Make this the focus as you gather around your lighted altar and once
again commit yourselves to His will!
Assign the following verses to highlight in their Bibles and to record in
their journals.

Psalm 143:4
Psalm 61:1-3
Psalm 46:1

Encourage each child to spend some quality time with the Lord in
prayer in their secret place, using the prayer in their journal (also on
page 69) to seek the Lord with.

Day 19

Putting it into Practice

Today we are going to focus on anointing oil and how to use it. Look up the following verses on anointing oil together and talk about them. Have children highlight them in their Bibles and take turns reading them out loud. They can later copy them into their journals during their secret place time.

James 5:14-15
Psalm 23:5
Isaiah 61:3
Hebrews 1:8-9

Anoint means to pour oil upon or to rub with oil, to consecrate, or set apart for Holy purposes.
In **Exodus 30:30** Aaron and his sons were anointed as priests to minister to the Lord in the Tent of Meeting or Tabernacle.
1 Samuel 16:12-13 tells of David being anointed as king.
Luke 7:36-50 is the story of the sinful woman anointing Jesus's feet with expensive perfume.
And **John 9:11** is the account of Jesus anointing the blind man's eyes with mud, thus restoring his sight.
As we see, oil (usually olive oil with spices in it), perfume and mud were all used for anointing for the purpose of consecrating to an office, forgiveness of sins, and healing. We are told in **James 5:14-15** to anoint and pray for one another for the purpose of healing and cleansing from sins.

Isaiah 61:3 tells us to wear the oil of joy instead of mourning.

Have a special time of blessing as you anoint each child with oil and pray God's grace and comfort to them. To do this, put a small dab of oil on your finger and rub on the forehead as you pray over the child. This is one of the most important things we can do for our children, to consecrate them to the Lord, acknowledging that they are His and to ask Him for wisdom and discernment in helping them to become all that He has called them to be.

We placed this jar of anointing oil and the altar on a tray as a centerpiece for the table. It is a good conversation piece when visitors come and a constant reminder of the lessons we're learning on this journey. Also use the oil to put on "boo-boos" and pray for healing, teaching young ones to go to the Lord with their hurts and tears.

This has been a very special day! I forgot to mention you might need a box of tissues as you share with your family this intimate moment in the Lord's mighty presence!

Day 20

Read aloud page 70 thru the middle of page 76

Putting it into Practice

Give each child stone #5 with the words, **"Bearing with Love"** written on one side and **"Forgiveness"** on the other side.
Also, give the corresponding card to put in their pouches.

Discuss forgiving, choosing to love, and becoming whom God wants you to be even when others are mean or hurtful to you. Let children discuss this issue, sharing concerns they have about hurtful people in their lives, even how they hurt each other as siblings. Reveal to them that God hurts when we hurt and He is also hurt when we choose to hurt someone else. He feels our pain with us.

Add a red flower to your vase with the yellow flower in it. Put this on the centerpiece tray in the middle of your table. Review the lessons learned by the flowers. Commit these lessons to prayer, either together or privately in their secret places.

Day 21

Today read from the middle of page 76-77.

Putting it into Practice

Stone #6 is to be given at this time. It is to be labeled **"Faith."**
Card #6 says, **"Whatever path you lead me on, I will not fear because You are with me."**

Sometimes we know the path ahead of us is not something we want to do and we have yet to see much progress spiritually. Then is the time to pause and allow the Lord to strengthen our faith and keep our focus on Him before we proceed. Kneel yet again at His altar and recommit our whole being to Him, trusting He alone can see into our hearts and knows full well the work He is doing in us, even if we don't see any outward signs of change yet.
Gather again around your altar and pray to the God who knows it all and loves you so very much! How blessed He is that you are seeking Him so deeply and wanting His way and not your own!

Suggested Song to Sing: **"It is the Cry of My Heart"**

Day 22

Do the "Think About It" section on page 78.

Recap the last 2 stones and their meanings. Why, after we've been hurt by someone, do we need to recommit to the Lord? (Give time for thought and response.) We need to totally release ourselves from the pain and to forgive and move on. If we don't we hit a road block spiritually and we will not progress until we deal with the hurt and unforgiveness. Why? Because God will not forgive us until we forgive others. See **Matthew 6:14-15.**

Discuss the memory verse and its meaning before going to their secret places. While there, write the memory verse, **Romans 12:21** on a card. Record it and **Matthew 6:14-15** in their journals. Also, highlight them in their Bibles. Say the prayer alone during this time. Put the memory card in a prominent place in your house to help you remember. Examples would be to put it in the kitchen window, or tape it to the bathroom mirror. Wear it around your neck on a string, etc.

<u>Supplies needed for Chapter 5</u>

> **a nice candle per person**
> **large marshmallows**
> **sticks to roast them on**

Day 23

Chapter 5
"To Full Surrender"

Read aloud page 79-88

Can you name the characters on pages 80-81?

Discuss the "Think About It" section on page 89 and 90.

Highlight in Bibles and record Bible verses on page 89 in journals.

Hopefully by now you can see and encourage your children that we are learning God's way of dealing with Pride, Resentment, Bitterness, and Self-Pity in our lives. We are learning that Sorrow and Suffering can do a mighty work in our hearts and that we can trust God with our lives as we surrender ourselves to Him. The peace of God will flow through our hearts and joy will radiate from our faces as we learn these valuable truths. Remind them to pray the prayer in their journals while in their secret places. Try singing a new song to the Lord!

Take some time to read through the next lesson before presenting it to the children. You will need to make some preparations to find and prepare a dark place to meet. A closet or basement room would be great unless you choose to do this one in the evening thus only needing to turn out the lights. You will need the candles, marshmallows, and roasting sticks for this lesson.

Day 24

Read aloud starting at page 91, pausing on page 93 where Much-Afraid empties her pouch.

Take this time to empty your pouches and recount the lessons you have learned.

Do you agree with Much-Afraid to keep these tokens of God's promises and continue on?

You will be blessed abundantly if you do!

Resume reading through page 96.

"Think about It"

Putting it into Practice

At this time give each child a candle. Find a dark place in your home representing the "Canyon of Full Surrender." Pray silently in the dark, surrendering your all and when each is finished, light his own candle, signifying that God is consuming his heartfelt prayer and that he is giving his all to God. Keep all the candles burning in the center of your group, hold hands and pray together asking God to make this real in

your lives and to help you continue to stay focused on Him.
Roast some marshmallows over the flames of your candles. Notice how the flames change the marshmallow and even start it on fire. Enjoy this special treat realizing the flames of God's love are changing you and consuming you. You are a sweet-smelling aroma to our Lord as you yield your life to Him.

Assign **Romans 12:1** and **Luke 6:46** to be highlighted and recorded in their journals. If you approve, allow the older ones to light their candles in their secret places and pray the prayer in their journals. It is also recorded on page 97.

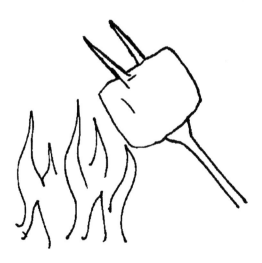

Day 25

Spend this day recapping the verses they wrote in their journals yesterday. Encourage and praise your children for how far they have come on this journey. Remind them that we are nearing the High Places and coming to the end of our journey. Ask them to share their favorite moments and why they are so special to them. Share your testimony with them about what God has taught you as well. Sing some worship songs if you like. Plan a special meal or dessert together. Prepare in prayer as a family for the rest of this journey. We want God to do a completed work in us! This would be a good time to review their journal work. We haven't done this yet. All that hard work has planted God's Word in our hearts and familiarized us with who He is and how much He loves us and wants to lead us and take care of us.

However the Lord leads, make this a special day! Be sure to tell Dad all the wonderful things you are learning if he is unable to be a part of this.

Supplies needed for Chapter 6

6 jewels per child of various colors (found at a craft store)
(They have a flat back and a multi-facet front)
poster board for the crowns (preferably gold)
(see instructions for crown on page 49)

<u>**Please read Chapter 6 before presenting it to your children and before reading any further.**</u>

Spend some quality time seeking the Lord on behalf of each child before this next lesson! This is the very special task I told you about at the beginning of this book. I would even recommend both parents praying together for this if possible. Ask God how He sees your little ones and what name He would give them to encourage them in their walk with Him. You will be putting these new names on their crowns after they make them.

As an example to you,

Our son, then age 11, was fearful of many things and he also would act silly to the point of annoyance at times. The Lord gave us the name "Wisdom and Valor" for him.

Our daughter, then age 9, loved to sing but would easily become upset with her little sister whom she shared a small bedroom with. The Lord called her "Peaceful Praise."

Our youngest daughter, then 2, is seven years younger than her older sister. She thinks she can do anything the big ones can do and doesn't like to be told differently. She can be strong-willed at times. It seemed the Lord told us to call her "Surrendered Obedience."

After pondering these names and "Grace and Glory's" new name I realized God sees us as He wants us to become. We often possess the opposite character qualities that when yielded to Him are changed completely around. This is the whole profound theme of the story of <u>Hinds' Feet on High Places</u>. These names for our children not only greatly encouraged them and challenged them to live up to the name, it focused us on our job as parents to channel them in the right direction. It gave us a goal to aim for in training them as they grow up and specific guidance for each child.

I pray the Lord will bless you as you seek Him on behalf of each child he has placed in your care and that you will hear clearly the names He has for them!

Prior to this next lesson replace the stones in each child's pouch with jewels, one per stone. What a surprise when you send them for their pouches or present them to each child and they find the jewels in them instead of the stones! I hope this is as much fun for the children as it is for Mom to prepare this. At least it was for me!

Day 26

Chapter 6
"Hinds' Feet on High Places"

Read pages 99 thru 103
Discuss the "Think About It" section on page 104

Putting it into Practice

Present the pouches to the children at this time! After they open them revealing what is inside, explain to them that their hard work has paid off and that their stones have been turned to jewels as a result of it. The work we do in serving the Lord is as jewels that we will put in our heavenly crowns when we meet Jesus face to face one day soon! What are our crowns for? The Bible says we will cast them at Jesus' feet to honor him!

Now for the fun part! We get to make crowns to wear and decorate them with these jewels. (See instructions on page 49.)

Explain that there is one more big set of important verses you would like them to record in their journals and highlight in their Bibles. Mom, if this is too much, choose only a few that mean the most to you. At least look them all up in their Bibles and highlight them and read them out loud together.

Phillipians 1:6

Psalm 30:5

Esther 9:22

Isaiah 54:11-12

Revelation 3:11

2 Timothy 2:12

Aren't you glad you didn't give up when you were tempted to before jumping into the Canyon of Full Surrender? The journey is so worth it!

Pray the prayer in your journals and on page 105 together.

Mom, find a secret time when you can put the new names on each crown without the children knowing about it. Ask the Lord to give you some scriptures that reinforce the name He gave to each child and have them ready to present to them tomorrow.

Day 27

Review the verses written in their journals yesterday. Talk about how God's people rejoiced when God brought them through a long and difficult journey.

Give them their crowns with their new names on them at this time. Make it special, ministering to each child individually and perhaps privately. Spend time sharing how the Lord gave you these names and what it means to them and to you!

Finish reading the book. Pages 107-114
Do the "Think About It" section.

Assign these few final verses for their journals. And memorize **Habakkuk 3:19**, the "theme verse" for this story.

2 Corinthians 1:4

John 7:38

Habakkuk 3:19

Pray the final prayer in the book!

Day 28

Examine yesterday's verses together!

Encourage children to continue to use their secret places to seek the Lord daily on their own. Ask them to share with God and with you their struggles and their victories! Maybe you could give a special keepsake box to each child to keep their stuff in from this journey!

Remember the Water Song throughout this book! Reread it on page 113. And the flowers' song on page 25 . . . it is so sweet to give and give. The water flows to the lowest places to water and nourish. Our Lord came to the lowest place to save us from the eternal death of sin. The flower song is to remind us and encourage us to give what we have, to share with others and to bloom where God has planted us. The purpose God has in taking us to the High Places is so that we, like the water, can return to the valley to tell others about Jesus great love for everyone!

Pray together, asking God how you can help water the world with your testimony of His love and forgiveness to you, to bloom where he has planted you and submit to His sovereign will for your lives!

Part Two

Instruction

&

Journal Pages

How to make the pouch.

Cut a piece of scrap fabric approximately 20" long and 7" wide. Cut the fabric for the pocket about 4 ½" long and 3 ½" wide. Fold the bottom and sides of the pockets under 1/4" and the top under 1/4" and then again ½". Sew to the outside of the cloth folding the cloth in half to position it toward the bottom center, pin the pocket in place after unfolding and stitch in place. Next fold the piece of material, right sides together joining top and bottom together. Stitch the side seams. Turn under the top 1/4" and then 1" again and stitch forming a casing. Also stitch 1/4' from the top. Make a hole in one of the side seams between the two casing stitches with a seam ripper. Feed a 20" string or ribbon through the casing and tie the two ends in a knot. Pull the string tight closing the top of the pouch. Keep cards in outside pocket of the pouch and stones inside the pouch.

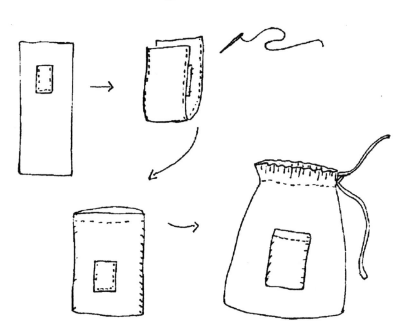

Other optional sources for pouches would be to cut off an old pants leg, sew the bottom shut and hem the top. Attach a string or cord to the top. A marble bag or something similar works too!

How to make the altar.

We turned a candle holder upside down on a snack plate and piled stones around it placing a tea light on top of the candle holder. We were then able to dismantle it when we were finished. If you want a more permanent altar you could hot-glue or mud the stones as you lay them around an object that would act as a stand for the tea light and put it on some kind of plate or flat object. Make sure the tea light is not secured so you can easily change it.

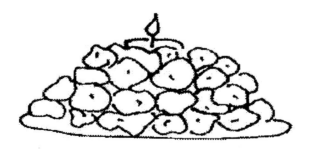

How to make the crown.

Using poster board, gold looks best if you can find it, cut out crowns similar to the illustration and adjust size to fit child's head. Cutting a slot on the right side and then adjusting to fit the size of head before cutting the slot on the left side insures a snug fit. We found that hot-gluing the jewels to the crown worked best. They seemed to fall off with other types of glue.

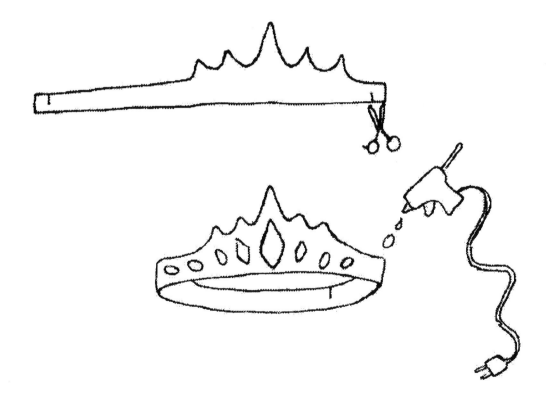

The following pages are for Mom to journal her thoughts and prayers as she leads her children on this journey.

Use them as examples to create your children's journals as well.

_____

_____

_____

_____

_____

_____

_____

_____

_____

_____

_____

_____

_____

_____

_____

_____

_____

"Jesus, sometimes I too am 'Much-Afraid.' Help me to trust You as my Shepherd. Please help my spirit-man not to be crippled and afraid. I want to be strong on the inside for You. As I read these chapters, please help me understand what they mean. Let the words make pictures in my heart of what lessons You want me to learn. Bye for now!"

_____

_____

_____

_____

_____

_____

_____

_____

_____

_____

_____

_____

_____

_____

"Jesus, You know all about me. You know what enemies come into my cottage, in my heart. Please help me keep the door locked, and not to let them in! When I do meet them, help me not to listen to them, but to call for Your help right away! And Lord, please help me spend time with You every day in my 'Secret Place." Bye for now"

"Thank You, Lord, for how You suffered for me. When things happen that hurt me or make me feel sad, please help me to trust You. Use the Sorrow and Suffering that I meet to make my spirit-man stronger. Amen."

My Journal - Day 6

My Prayer List

_____

_____

_____

_____

_____

_____

_____

_____

_____

_____

_____

_____

_____

_____

_____

_____

_____

_____

_____

_____

_____

"Oh, Lord! Help me not to listen to Pride. Help me not to worry about what other people think of me. I want my life to please You. I want to depend on You for everything. I know I can't make it through this life unless You go with me, but with You by my side, I can do all things! (Like make friends, pass tests, obey my parents, clean my room . . . .)"

My Journal - Day 14

<u>*My Journal - Day 15*</u>

_____

_____

_____

_____

_____

_____

_____

_____

_____

_____

_____

_____

_____

_____

"Oh, Jesus, when bad or hard things happen to me, help me not to get upset and complain. Help me to be Acceptance-With-Joy, and to trust that You are looking after me. You are making me into the person You want me to be. I don't want to be like a lump of hard, dry play dough! I want to be soft clay in Your hands. And I don't want to just be a rock.
I want to be a precious stone, pure gold for You. Help me to rejoice when I go through a 'fiery trial'! Amen."

My Journal - Day 17

_____
_____
_____
_____
_____
_____
_____
_____
_____
_____
_____
_____
_____
_____
_____

"Lord, You know what goes on inside my head. You know how hard it is for me to trust You when it looks like You aren't with me, or when it seems as if You aren't going to answer my prayers. Help me not to just look at what I see with me eyes. Teach me to walk by faith trusting You. Your ways are higher than mine. You will do what is right and good for me, though not always the way I think You should. Help me not to listen to Pride, Resentment, Bitterness, or Self-Pity. Help me to fill my head and heart with Your words and listen to what You say! Bye for Now!"

_____

_____

_____

_____

_____

_____

_____

_____

_____

_____

_____

_____

_____

_____

_____

_____

"Oh, Lord, when I feel as though my heart is 'overwhelmed,' help me to spend time in my 'secret place' with You. Help me to cry out my feelings, so they don't just stay inside me. Help me to give You my fears, doubts, and worries. Thank You for being my heavenly Daddy. Thank You for Your big, strong arms that I can run to."

My Journal - Day 19

_____
_____
_____
_____
_____
_____
_____
_____
_____
_____
_____
_____
_____
_____
_____
_____

"Bearing-With-Love is a hard lesson to learn, Lord. Help! When someone does wrong to me, I want to fight back. Help me to do good to those who hurt me. Help me to be like You. You forgave the people who nailed You to the cross. You still forgive people who hurt You. You bless and help people who don't deserve it. Wow! You are really awesome! Bye for now."

_____

_____

_____

_____

_____

_____

_____

_____

_____

_____

_____

_____

_____

_____

"Thank You for Your peace, Lord Jesus. I want it to be in my heart all day, every day. No matter what is happening - at school, in my family, with my friends - help me to choose to let Your peace rule. You are my hiding place. You will keep me safe in the stormy times of my life. Help me not to worry or get upset; help me to sing praises from my heart to You!"

_____

_____

_____

_____

_____

_____

_____

_____

_____

_____

_____

_____

_____

_____

_____

_____

_____

_____

"Thank You, Jesus, for this wonderful story. Thank You that the Canyon of Full Surrender is a beautiful, peaceful place. Making You Lord and Master of my whole life is the best thing that I could ever do. Oh Jesus, be my Savior and be my Lord. Amen."

_____

_____

_____

_____

_____

_____

_____

_____

_____

_____

_____

_____

_____

_____

_____

_____

"Lord, You see each time I lay down my own desires and do what You want . . . each time I learn to trust You as I walk on my path . . . each act of service and surrender. And You are collecting precious stones for the crown I will wear someday. Thank You for the work You are doing in my spirit-man. Thank You for changing my Much-Afraid heart into a heart that is beautiful and strong for You. Bye for now!"

"The world sure is in lots of trouble, Lord. People everywhere are going through really hard times. They need your help! Help me to live on the High Places where I can better see things the way You do. Please use my life. Let me be like that waterfall. Let me pour out to others what You give to me. Help me every day to spend time with You in my Secret Place. Make my spirit-man powerful so I don't spend my life limping and struggling. I want to spend my life filled with Your strength to help others. I love You, Lord! Bye for now."

My Journal

_____

_____

_____

_____

_____

_____

_____

_____

_____

_____

_____

_____

_____

_____

_____

_____

_____

_____

_____

_____

_____

_____

_____

My Journal

My Journal

_____

_____

_____

_____

_____

_____

_____

_____

_____

_____

_____

_____

_____

_____

_____

_____

_____

_____

_____

_____

_____

1st Stone: I lay down my desires. I will trust You, Lord, to choose what is best for me.

2nd Stone: Acceptance-With-JOY
Whatever the Lord lets me go through, I want to trust Him and allow Him to have His way in my life. And I want to do it with joy in my heart!

3rd Stone: I will wait patiently until the Lord does what He said He will do.

4th Stone: I lay down my will, and desire to do what I want, so I can do Your will and what You want me to do, Lord,

5th Stone:
Bearing-With-Love
No matter how I am hurt or mistreated, I will choose to forgive and love.

6th Stone: Whatever path You lead me on, I will not fear, because You are with me.